Here are some other nonfiction chapter books you will enjoy:

Caves!: Underground Worlds
by Jeanne Bendick

Earthworms: Underground Farmers
by Patricia Lauber

Exploring an Ocean Tide Pool
by Jeanne Bendick

Frozen Girl
by David Getz

Frozen Man
by David Getz

Great Whales: The Gentle Giants
by Patricia Lauber

In Search of the Grand Canyon:
Down the Colorado with John Wesley Powell
by Mary Ann Fraser

Life on Mars
by David Getz

Lighthouses: Watchers at Sea
by Brenda Z. Guiberson

Robots Rising
by Carol Sonenklar

Salmon Story
by Brenda Z. Guiberson

Spotted Owl: Bird of the Ancient Forest
by Brenda Z. Guiberson

Tales of the Haunted Deep
by Brenda Z. Guiberson

Vicksburg: The Battle That Won the Civil War
by Mary Ann Fraser

MUMMY MYSTERIES

TALES FROM NORTH AMERICA

BRENDA Z. GUIBERSON

A REDFEATHER CHAPTER BOOK

HENRY HOLT AND COMPANY
NEW YORK

To all my writer and illustrator friends
who continually fill me with
creative ideas and wisdom.

Thanks to all the people who helped get this book through its
various phases, including Margaret Garrou and many others at
Holt, and Joyce M. Raab, who shared the Chaco Culture Archives.

Henry Holt and Company, LLC, *Publishers since 1866*
115 West 18th Street, New York, New York 10011

Henry Holt is a registered trademark of Henry Holt and Company, LLC

Library of Congress Cataloging-in-Publication Data
Guiberson, Brenda Z. Mummy mysteries: tales from North America /
Brenda Z. Guiberson. p.   cm. — (A Redfeather Book)
Includes bibliographical references and index.
Summary: Presents various accounts of mummies found throughout North America
and what these bodies reveal about the times in which they lived.
1. Mummies—Juvenile literature.   2. Mummies—North America—
Juvenile literature. [1. Mummies.] I. Title. II. Series: Redfeather Books.
GN293.G85   1998   393'.3—dc21   97-50428

ISBN 0-8050-5369-7   First Edition—1998   Designed by Meredith Baldwin
Printed in Mexico
3 5 7 9 10 8 6 4 2

CONTENTS

Gift 8-10-11 cow

A BRIEF HISTORY
OF MUMMIES

MUMMIES ARE REAL. They have been found in such diverse places as mountains, caves, ice, and bogs, but they all have something in common. The mummified bodies have been protected from water, oxygen, and insects so that decay of soft body tissues cannot begin. Sometimes this is deliberate. Mummies found in Alaska, for instance, were cleaned, dried, and then protected by sea lion guts from water damage. Other mummies have been pickled in arsenic, seared in the hot sun, and even smoked in the way that meat is turned into jerky.

Some mummies have been preserved naturally when they were buried in thick mud or smothered in peat bogs. These were protected from oxygen. Some bog mummies in Europe still have eyelashes and delicate fin-

Mummies found in European bogs are some of the best preserved.

gerprints after 2,000 years. Other mummies were freeze-dried in cold places or lost their moisture in dry caves or deserts. These were protected from decay caused by moisture. Even small things like insects can become mummified. The resin, or sap, that dripped from ancient trees sometimes trapped insects, plants, feathers, and even small tree frogs. Some of these drippings hardened into amber, which was preserved for millions of years.

The most famous mummy makers, the Egyptians, first buried their dead in graves beneath the hot desert sands. With the high temperatures and low humidity, the bodies dried out so quickly that they became natural mummies. The Egyptians liked this unexpected result. They believed that after death the spirit traveled to another world and needed to recognize its body in order to return. This traveling back and forth allowed the person to live forever. The Egyptians decided to make mummies themselves and perfected this art over the next 3,000 years.

With the natural mummies in mind, the Egyptians knew they had to dry out the bodies. They first removed the moist inside organs, where decay would begin. The intestines, stomach, liver, and lungs were dried in separate containers and later placed in the tomb with the mummy. At times the Egyptians even pulled out the brains with a hook through the nostrils. Then they covered the bodies with a natural salt called natron. The natron absorbed all the moisture from the corpse. Since a body is over 70 percent water, a dried-out corpse has lost a lot of weight.

Sometimes the Egyptians coated the mummies with tree resin, which sealed out oxygen, bacteria, water, and tiny insects. As the dried-out bodies turned dark and brittle they were wrapped with up to eighty layers of linen cloth

This dehydrated mummy found in Colorado weighs just sixteen pounds.

A woolly mammoth buried under the ice quickly freezes, and it becomes a mummy.

for further protection. In this long process, which took about seventy days, the Egyptians got what they wanted—a body that could be recognized for thousands of years.

Over time, the Egyptians apparently made millions, perhaps hundreds of millions, of mummies! And because the Egyptians felt that gods and goddesses were connected to different animals, they also mummified millions of animals, including ibises, crocodiles, cats, monkeys, snakes, fish, falcons, bulls, and even insects.

Mummies have been deliberately made in such diverse places as Peru, China, Austria, and Italy. But in North America, the largest number of mummies occur as a rare accident of nature. They still have all their organs in place and are the best preserved of all. They are usually surrounded by fascinating items from their time—clothing, weapons, food, and tools. An archaeologist explained it this way: "One finds the little things that bring back the ancient life with startling vividness . . . a stirring stick still smeared with cornmeal mush, a patched sandal, a cake of salt wrapped in corn husk."

Mummification has helped us discover some of the health problems of the past, many of which continue to affect people today. Some mummies show evidence of carbon particles in their lungs caused by air pollution that existed around smoky fires. Other health problems that have shown up in mummies are ear and tooth infections, clogged arteries, malnutrition, polio, and arthritis. Smallpox can be identified from scars on the face. Eight mummies from caves in Arizona were found with lice still preserved in their hair.

A natural mummy found in Peru dates from 500 years before Columbus came to America. An autopsy revealed that this mummy had tubercu-

Insects have been found mummified in sap that dripped from ancient trees. When dried, the sap is called amber.

Sacred Egyptian animals mummified:

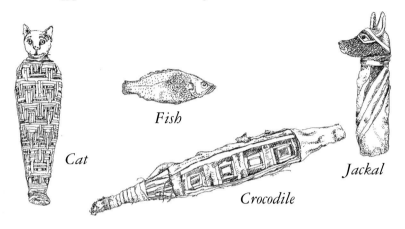

Cat

Fish

Crocodile

Jackal

losis lumps in her lungs. Before this discovery, it was thought that tuberculosis was a disease brought to the New World by European travelers. This information has changed our ideas about how this disease spread around the world. A 2,000-year-old mummy from China died of a heart attack and was buried with herbal medicines for heart disease. Now we know that heart disease is not caused only by modern eating and living habits.

Whether mummies are of people, animals, or insects, they always reveal something about their ancient life and environment. If we look carefully at the clues they provide, mummies can solve mysteries from the past.

THE MYSTERIOUS
MUMMIES OF THE
ALEUTIAN ISLANDS

ISLANDS OF THE FOUR MOUNTAINS, Alaska, 1928.
Harold McCracken is on a small island in Alaska looking
for mummies. As leader of an expedition for the American Museum of Natural History, he has brought a whole
crew to one of the stormiest and most dangerous places
on earth. They have searched every cave for mummies
without success. McCracken is worried. Didn't he gather
enough clues over the last eleven years to find them? Do
Alaskan mummies really exist, or has he just been enter-
tained with a few tall tales from the north?

It was a mate on an Alaskan ship who first told
McCracken about mummies in the Aleutian Islands. He
said the mummies would be "chiefs or famous whale
hunters, fixed up just like the ones they get in

Egypt . . . long before the first Russians came over here." And from another source the most important clue: "The Islands of the Four Mountains is [*sic*] the only place they put them."

McCracken's life has been filled with adventure since he got interested in mummies. He has been in a shipwreck, lost some toenails to frostbite, hunted for grizzly bear, and traded his six-shooter to an old chief for more stories of mummies. He is a scientist who wants to learn more about how people first migrated to the New World. Did they use the Aleutian Islands as stepping-stones, or did they travel only across the land bridge that

Map of the Aleutian Islands of Alaska. Arrows show how people might have migrated to the New World.

connected Asia and the New World during the Ice Age? If Asians came to the islands, when was it, and how many times? He writes that a study of artifacts from an ancient island culture might have a "definite and important bearing upon that subject."

McCracken searched until he ran out of his own money. Then he sold fox skins and magazine articles and ate caribou meat three times a day to keep going. He even had a job controlling cockroaches in a ship's galley. Now he finally has museum experts and good equipment to help with this search, but will they ever discover a mummy?

Junius Bird, the botanist on the team, calls to him from the rocky cliff: "I've found a log cabin." McCracken is surprised. Big trees do not grow on the volcanic, stormy Aleutian Islands. The nearest forest is 800 miles away. He hurries to investigate and sees a "row of age-rotted logs carefully placed there by human hands." He calls everyone over, and soon the expedition members are digging through the dirt and taking pictures of everything they remove.

Under the logs they find a layer of tightly woven grass matting. With hours of digging they uncover tanned sealskins. Below that are more logs, more mats, and more skins. It is clear that someone has made a great effort to pile up all of these layers. McCracken says he could not be more excited if he were looking for pirate gold.

They keep digging. Next they uncover sea lion guts, expertly sewn together into tight waterproof sheets. Then they find a boat paddle for a lightweight, skin-covered boat called a *bidarka,* which was used by the great whale and seal hunters. There is also a stone lamp to burn whale or seal oil for light, cooking, and heat.

Below that is a chamber where the team makes a startling discovery. They uncover a "dry brown, wrinkled hand . . . the hand of a Stone Age human mummy of the Arctic."

The Aleuts hunted for whales in thirty-pound, skin-covered boats called bidarkas.

An Aleut woman carries dried and inflated seal gut to be made into waterproof parkas. A seal-gut parka with drawstrings.

McCracken is amazed. Has he found a *toja,* a great whale hunter and chief? Gradually they uncover the whole body. The man is wearing a "beautiful parka of sea otter trimmed with bird skins." Like a hunter, he has a harpoon, a spear, a wooden shield, and a cone-shaped hat. Extra skins surround him—from pup seals, sea otters, and a seabird decorated with designs and red coloring.

The mummies in the second chamber include a man, a woman, a young child, and a baby, perhaps killed to accompany the chief. The adults are clothed in more simple sealskin parkas and hoods. The man may be a bodyguard. The woman is a seamstress with a sealskin bag full of tools and materials to sew for the great chief. Her body has slipped into a wet corner and decayed, but a waterproof gut hood still protects and preserves her head. She has beads dangling from her nose, and four of them are made of amber.

According to stories McCracken has been told, the spirits of whale hunters "leave their hard dried bodies and fly out to sea to pursue the ponderous whale." The team can see that the Aleuts worked very hard to preserve these bodies. Their inside organs have been removed and replaced with straw. Round clumps of brown clay replace the eyeballs, and the fingernails have been pulled out. Weyer, the archaeologist, reports that "the Aleut mummy was in a better state of preservation than most of those he had seen during his work . . . in Egypt."

No metal tools or woven cloth are found with the mummies, and all the log cutting has been done with stone tools. Because of this, McCracken thinks the mummies are very old, made before the first Russian traders came to the area in the early 1700s. But the most important part of the discovery for McCracken is the four amber beads found with the seamstress mummy. McCracken and a museum curator believe the amber is

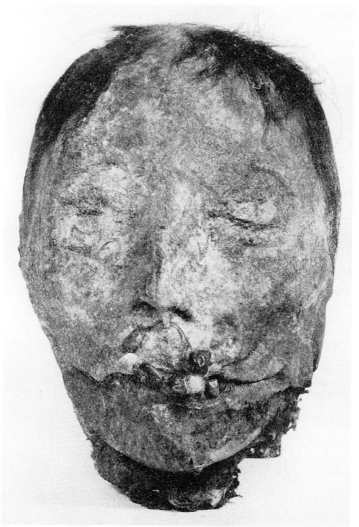

Mummified head of Aleut woman with beads of Korean amber.
Neg. no. 338632, courtesy Department of Library Services, American
Museum of Natural History.

from a tree resin found only in Korea—3,000 miles away. This indicates contact between an old island culture and Asia. But how long ago? And who brought the amber to the Aleutian Islands?

In 1928 McCracken could not fully answer these questions, and today much is still uncertain. But the mummy discovery helps us learn more about the great whale hunters and the respect given them by their people. The materials preserved with the mummies reveal a clever ability to make tools and clothing from the environment that are just right for survival on cold, stormy seas.

Mummies with rare and unusual materials that tell us about ancient lives have been found all over the world. They are like time capsules guarding mysterious information that may never be discovered in any other way. To investigate a mummy mystery, it helps to understand how mummies are made and how to read their ancient clues.

THE MYSTERY
OF BLUE BABE

PEARL CREEK, ALASKA, 1979. A gold miner with a powerful jet of water is washing out a frozen dirt bank. Ice-cold streams of mud dribble down the slope as he blasts away with his hose. After a while he begins to uncover something, but it is not the gold he is looking for. It is a hoof, belonging to a frozen animal buried deep in the mud. It has hair, muscles, hide, and horns. Is it important? Unusual? The miner thinks so. He asks scientists to investigate, and a mummy mystery begins to unfold.

The animal turns out to be a huge bison partially eaten before it froze. Because of its position buried under multiple layers of soil and peat, the scientists can tell that it is very, very old—36,000 years old. This takes it back to the time of the Pleistocene, when humans first

Gold miner Walter Roman demonstrates the hose he was using when he found Blue Babe. Photo: R. Dale Guthrie.

appeared. The animal is covered with blue crystals formed in the damp silt. A big blue bison? They decide to call him Blue Babe after Paul Bunyan's great blue ox.

Carefully they extract Blue Babe from the frozen ground and then preserve him in a huge walk-in freezer at the University of Alaska. They also freeze bags and buckets of the silt dug out around him so they can study it for hairs, pollen, and other samples. Already Blue Babe is an exciting find. Bison no longer live in the far north, but this animal managed to survive there 36,000 years ago. How did he live, and then how did he die? As a mummy, Blue Babe leaves extra clues behind to tell a story.

Tooth wear and the rings on his horns reveal that he was about eight years old. Food particles in his teeth show that he was a grazer and ate willow and grasses. The particles even show that he ate a grass called *Danthonia,* which no longer grows in the area where he was found.

Blue Babe also had thick underfur and a layer of fat. This means he was killed in the fall or early winter as the bison grew extra fur and ate large amounts of food to prepare for the long, cold winter.

But it is the preserved hide that leads to the most amazing discovery. There are long claw marks scratched onto the rear and the hind legs of Blue Babe and small punctures from teeth. What attacked this bison and

Blue Babe: a mystery 36,000 years old. Photo: Barnet McWayne, for University of Alaska Museum.

tried to pull it down with sharp claws? It had to be a large animal because Blue Babe was huge and could defend himself with his horns.

The scientists look up information about teeth and claws of possible predators. They decide the marks didn't come from a bear because bear claws are used for digging and are not so sharp. It wasn't a wolf because wolves don't use their claws to catch prey. It wasn't a saber-toothed tiger because its serrated teeth could rip open the hide like a knife and would not leave shallow punctures like those found on Blue Babe.

Are there any more clues? The scientists note the clotted blood around Blue Babe's snout and the puncture marks and scratches on his head, in combination with the injuries on the animal's rear. These mummy clues point to one large animal that tried to pull Blue Babe down from behind while another grabbed his head. This is the way lions hunt. Did lions live in the far north with Blue Babe 36,000 years ago?

The scientists go back to research. They study cave paintings from other parts of the world from the Pleistocene to get clues about how bison and lions looked and behaved in this time. Lions were usually painted in

What killed Blue Babe? The clues:

A saber-toothed tiger canine tooth can slice through hide.

Lion claws are very sharp.

Bear claws are worn down from digging.

A lion canine makes punctures like those found on Blue Babe.

Wolf canines

Lion canines

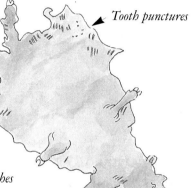

Scratches

Tooth punctures

The width between puncture wounds matches the width between a lion's canines, about 3.5 inches (almost 9 centimeters). A wolf's canines are just over 1.5 inches (4 centimeters) wide and too small to make these punctures.

Blue Babe's hide has puncture wounds and scratches at both front and back.

Today's lions attack large animals from the front and the back.

small groups of two or three, not in large prides as seen today. Whereas a large pride of lions would have finished off Blue Babe quickly, he was only partially eaten before his body froze and became hard. This shows that there were probably just two lions that made the kill.

The final evidence that clinches the lion theory comes when the scientists work to restore Blue Babe for display at the University of Alaska Museum. In the mummified tissue of the bison's muscle is a chipped piece of tooth. They are able to identify it as the tooth of a lion and know that lions were once able to survive in the far north. The mystery of Blue Babe's death is solved!

To reconstruct Blue Babe accurately, scientists studied ancient engravings and cave paintings.

Cave painting, Spain, 14,000 years old.

Engraved stone, France, 20,000 years old.

After the bison is cleaned up and restored, the scientists decide to celebrate. R. Dale Guthrie, one of the scientists, wrote, "A small part of the mummy's neck was diced and simmered in a pot of stock and vegetables. We had Blue Babe for dinner. The meat was well aged but still a little tough, and it gave the stew a strong Pleistocene aroma, but nobody there would have dared miss it."

A mummy frozen for 36,000 years retains an amazing amount of clues about its life and environment. But a mummy doesn't have to be that old to help us solve a mystery from the past.

Cave painting, France,
17,000 years old.

Blue Babe, Alaska,
36,000 years old.

THE MYSTERY OF
THE LOST EXPLORERS

ARCTIC EXPEDITION, 1845. Two expedition ships, the *Erebus* and the *Terror,* set sail in May from England on a dangerous mission. One hundred thirty-four elite sailors are aboard. Sir John Franklin, their leader, is confident they will succeed. He has more than thirty years' experience in polar explorations and once escaped starvation by eating his leather boots. For his distinguished service he has received many awards, including a gold medal from the Paris Geographical Society.

The expedition is looking for the Northwest Passage, a route that could take them from the Atlantic Ocean across the icy top of the world all the way to the Pacific Ocean. For three centuries explorers have failed to find such a passage through the maze of unmapped islands and frozen seas in the Arctic. But the Franklin Expedition is well stocked, and the sailors believe they will be the ones to succeed for Queen Victoria and the British Empire.

The bows of the ships are covered with heavy sheets of iron to cut through the ice. Hot-water pipes have been installed to warm the sleeping berths during the dark, frigid winters. There are almost 3,000 books to keep the sailors busy and research instruments to study the new

Map of the Franklin Expedition's route through the Arctic islands in search of the Northwest Passage. Arrows show the route.

and unknown things they will see. For the sailors' health, barrels and barrels of lemon juice have been brought aboard to protect them from scurvy, a sickness often experienced by sailors on long journeys without fresh fruit and vegetables.

They even bring along two new inventions of the time—a camera and food packed in tin cans. Stowed away are thousands of tins of prime meat, thick soups, and vegetables, all carefully sealed to prevent decay.

In July they reach Greenland. Sir John Franklin brags to the captain of a whaling ship that he has enough pro-

The Franklin Expedition ships, the Erebus *and the* Terror, *sail off into the icy seas, looking for the Northwest Passage.*

visions for five years and if necessary could "make them spin out for seven years." Then the ships sail west into Baffin Bay. While the rest of the world waits one year, two years, then three years, no further word is heard from the expedition.

By 1848 everyone is very worried. The English government and Sir John Franklin's wife offer huge rewards to anyone who can find and help the lost explorers. By 1850 there are fifteen ships and 500 men combing the Arctic. The searchers try to contact the expedition with everything from carrier pigeons to arctic foxes to hydrogen balloons. They even paint huge messages on cliffs.

Very few traces of the Franklin Expedition are found. After years of search, three marked graves and a huge pile of empty tin cans are discovered on remote Beechey Island, where the crew spent its first winter in 1846. John Torrington died in January at age twenty. John Hartnell died a few days later at age twenty-five. William Braine, age thirty-three, died in April. Many wonder why three young men died so early in the trip.

In 1857 Lieutenant Hobson finds a cairn, a heap of stones piled up as a memorial or marker, on King William Island. He and his men are excited because this

Lieutenant Hobson and his party breaking down the cairn.

cairn is just the place where the explorers would leave a message. Quickly they move the rocks and find a rusty metal cylinder. A fragile piece of paper with rust splotches is inside. It is a standard emergency statement written in six languages and signed by officers of the Franklin Expedition. Additional information is written all around the margins, stating that the ships were caught in ice and "Sir John Franklin died on the 11th June 1847 and the total loss by deaths in the Expedition has been to this date 9 officers and 15 men." The other survivors intend to cross the ice in search of a trading post on the Back River.

This "bottle paper" doesn't explain what happened to these survivors. It doesn't explain why so many officers

28 of May 1847

H. M. S.hips *Erebus* and *Terror*
{ Wintered in the Ice in
{ Lat. 70° 5′ N Long. 98° 23′ W

Having wintered in 1846—7 at Beechey Island
in Lat 74° 43′ 28″ N Long 91° 39′ 15″ W after having
ascended Wellington Channel to Lat 77° and returned
by the West side of Cornwallis Island

Commander.

Sir John Franklin commanding the Expedition

all well

WHOEVER finds this paper is requested to forward it to the Secretary of the Admiralty, London, *with a note of the time and place at which it was found*: or, if more convenient, to deliver it for that purpose to the British Consul at the nearest Port.

QUINCONQUE trouvera ce papier est prié d'y marquer le tems et lieu ou il l'aura trouvé, et de le faire parvenir au plutot au Secretaire de l'Amirauté Britannique à Londres.

CUALQUIERA que hallare este Papel, se le suplica de enviarlo al Secretario del Almirantazgo, en Londrés, con una nota del tiempo y del lugar en donde se halló.

EEN ieder die dit Papier mogt vinden, wordt hiermede verzogt, om hezelve, ten spoedigste, te willen zenden aan den Heer Minister van de Marine der Nederlanden in 's Gravenhage, of wel aan den Secretaris der Britsche Admiraliteit, te London, en daar by te voegen eene Nota, inhoudende de tyd en de plaats alwaar dit Papier is gevonden geworden.

FINDEREN af dette Papiir ombedes, naar Leilighed gives, at sende samme til Admiralitets Secretairen i London, eller nærmeste Embedsmand i Danmark, Norge, eller Sverrig. Tiden og Stædit hvor dette er fundet ønskes venskabeligt paategnet.

WER diesen Zettel findet, wird hier-durch ersucht denselben an den Secretair des Admiralitets in London einzusenden, mit gefälliger angabe an welchen ort und zu welcher zeit er gefunden worden ist.

Party consisting of 2 Officers and 6 Men
left the Ships on Monday 24th May 1847

Gm Gore Lieut
Chas F Des Voeux Mate

The message left in the cairn. Tacoma Public Library.

died when they had better quarters and better tinned food than the rest of the crew. And it doesn't say where Franklin is buried or where the ships might be.

A few more artifacts are found, including two skeletons that look as if they died trying to pull a heavy sleigh and boat across the frozen land. Are they the last of the group looking for the Back River? The boat is loaded with luxury items like curtain rods, soap, silk handkerchiefs, and slippers. None of these things would help them survive in the harsh Arctic climate. Why would they exhaust themselves dragging such a heavy and unnecessary load? Were they thinking clearly?

Despite these clues, the mystery remains unsolved. Then in 1981 Canadian scientists make a new discovery: scattered bones from a sailor on the expedition. With more modern ways to study them, the scientists find very high levels of lead in the bones, enough to cause weakness, confusion, and poor decisions. Lead poisoning can cause people to act in bizarre and unusual ways. Did this have anything to do with the fate of the expedition?

Lead can accumulate in bone anytime during a person's life. Maybe the sailor was exposed to lead as a child.

The scientists want to know if the sailor got it during the very last years of his life. Only strands of hair from someone on the expedition could provide this information. A mummy is needed to solve this mystery.

The scientists are aware of the three men, Torrington, Hartnell, and Braine, buried on ice-cold Beechey Island. Is it possible they were frozen quickly and preserved? After looking for relatives of the three, they manage to get government permission to dig them up in 1984, after the sailors had been buried for 138 years.

A group of scientists pack up tents, food, heaters, and an electric alarm fence to warn of wandering polar bears. Then they fly out to remote Beechey Island. Carefully they remove rocks from Torrington's grave and then spend two days chipping into the permafrost and pouring heated water over the ice. Eventually they smell the musty blue wool fabric covering the coffin. Then they see the perfectly preserved toes of John Torrington, the twenty-year-old leading stoker on the *Terror.* His job was to feed and tend the furnace of the steam engine, but instead he was the first to die on the expedition.

He wears gray linen trousers and a white shirt with blue stripes. A kerchief with blue polka dots is wrapped

Scientists on Beechey Island used photos and grids to reconstruct a grave. Copyright Owen Beattie, from *Frozen in Time/Buried in Ice,* reprinted by permission of Westwood Creative Artists.

around his head. He is so well preserved that his body is still soft and limp. His hands have no calluses, as if he had been unable to work for some time. He is a natural frozen mummy, very different from the stiff, leathery mummies of Egypt. No food is found in his stomach or intestines. He is so thin that he probably stopped eating long before he died. There is no layer of fat under his skin, and all his ribs can be seen.

Once the other two bodies are found, the scientists collect tissue, hair, fingernail, bone, and organ samples from all three bodies and rebury them exactly as they were. They also take a close look at the nearby pile of empty cans of food. The metal edges and seams are

John Torrington's frozen body was remarkably well preserved. Copyright Owen Beattie, from *Frozen in Time/ Buried in Ice,* reprinted by permission of Westwood Creative Artists.

sealed on the inside with thick lines of lead and tin solder dribbling down like honey.

Tests on the hair samples reveal that all three men had high levels of lead. This means that the lead had accumulated during the expedition. The lead also matches the lead in the solder (90 percent lead) in the tinned food, and there is enough in the three men's bodies to rob them of strength, appetite, and the ability to make good decisions. In their weakened condition, the men died of pneumonia and tuberculosis. And why did so many of the officers die early? Like these sick men, they were

The deadly solder seam of lead can still be seen on this tin. Copyright Owen Beattie, from *Frozen in Time/Buried in Ice,* reprinted by permission of Westwood Creative Artists.

probably given more of the special rations—the tinned food. The explorers were doomed by the very invention that was meant to nourish them.

Sir John Franklin's body has never been found. Bones from a few other crew members reveal even higher lead levels and also signs of scurvy, freezing, starvation, and perhaps even cannibalism. The toxic lead content in their diet most likely contributed to declining health, poor decisions, and the sad failure of the expedition.

British scientists in the mid-1800s were just beginning to understand the effects of lead poisoning. It took another forty-five years after the Franklin Expedition before food manufacturers were forbidden to solder cans on the inside.

THE DISAPPEARANCE OF
THE ANASAZI PEOPLE

ANCIENT DESERTED CITIES, Southwest United States, 1890s. Archaeologists, treasure hunters, and Navajo workers are sifting through the dirt of great cliff houses and cave dwellings of a past civilization just discovered. Even though the ruins have been abandoned for centuries, many artifacts are still preserved in this dry desert climate. Everywhere the workers find exciting evidence of the people they call the Anasazi, the "ancient ones."

At one site, in the back of a dry cave, they discover a mummified body sitting in a basket with another huge basket pulled over its head. Other mummies are found with sandals, flutes, pipes, squash seeds, digging sticks, and rabbit fur blankets. And everywhere there are bas-

Searching for artifacts in Pueblo Bonito. Neg. no. 411970, courtesy Department of Library Services, American Museum of Natural History.

kets, big and little ones, flat and round; baskets for cooking, carrying, and even a basket full of corn—a pile of dusty cobs untouched for more than a thousand years.

The preserved food reveals that these early people were changing their lives from wanderers looking for seeds and berries to farmers growing corn and squash. Farming gave them a reliable food supply and allowed them to stay in one place long enough to develop new skills and large communities.

Their earliest houses were simple pits in the ground, but the Anasazi were clever weavers. They used the yucca plant to weave sandals to protect their feet from the hot sand and cactus spines. They wove tight water baskets that did not leak. They wove long nets to catch rabbits

An Anasazi mummy. Neg. no. 310539, courtesy Department of Library Services, American Museum of Natural History.

for food and then twisted the rabbit fur with other materials to make warm blankets. Because of all this wonderful weaving, the earliest Anasazi are called "Basket Makers." They first came to the Southwest around A.D. 1.

Other digging and sifting by archaeologists reveal more mummies and clues to tell us how these people developed over the next few hundred years. They moved into bigger homes with rooms for storing crops and raising turkeys. They used grinding stones to prepare food from plants, and designed axes, hoes, hammers, and knives made from stones and animal bone. The children had toys such as a doll made from a cottonwood stick with curled cedar bark for the skirt.

Yucca sandals made by the Anasazi. Photo: Brenda Z. Guiberson, permission National Park Service, Chaco Culture NHP Museum

It is apparent that the Anasazi traded with other groups because items with more advanced technology are found in their homes. The Anasazi began to hunt with bows and arrows, which were far more efficient than the spear throwers, the *atlatls,* they used earlier. And they began to fill their homes with pottery. Because hard clay pots lasted a long time and were better for boiling water, they no longer made so many baskets.

The mummies reveal a lot about the health of the Anasazi. Scientists found carbon particles in their lungs that came from standing near fires that spewed smoke and ashes into the air. Their bones and muscles indicate that everyone, both men and women, shared in the hard physical labor. They also suffered from arthritis. Their teeth were worn down from eating corn that collected tiny bits of stone as it was ground. The children were

A spear thrown with a notched atlatl *will go farther than if thrown by hand.*

anemic and had poor tooth enamel because basic nutrients were missing in their high corn diet.

Around A.D. 700 the Anasazi began to build houses with several living areas and two or three storage rooms. Some of their greatest accomplishments occurred in Chaco Canyon, New Mexico. Here they built twelve great pueblo cities. One of them, Pueblo Bonito, became the largest apartment house in the world until a bigger one was built in New York City in 1882. The great stone walls of Pueblo Bonito were strong enough to support 800 rooms as high as five stories. The rooms were solar designed, collecting as much heat as possible from the winter sun.

Pueblo Bonito during its prime. National Park Service, Chaco Culture NHP Museum Collection.

One mummy found at Pueblo Bonito was wearing a necklace made with 2,500 turquoise beads. The Anasazi became masters of using turquoise, a blue-green stone mined from the nearby mountains. They also traded the valuable turquoise for exotic items from Mexico such as copper bells, conch shell trumpets, and macaws. The colorful bird feathers were woven into their clothing.

Anasazi engineers constructed 400 miles of roads to connect the communities. They also worked out an elaborate system of dams, canals, and ditches to water their crops. Not afraid of hard work, they hauled in 200,000

The ruins of Pueblo Bonito today. National Park Service, Chaco Culture NHP Museum Collection.

ponderosa pines from at least thirty miles away for all this construction. How they managed to move these heavy logs remains a mystery because they had no wheels, no metal tools, and no large animals to help them.

But the biggest mystery of all is why they suddenly left. By A.D. 1250 the Anasazi had abandoned cities all over the Southwest, leaving them to crumble slowly over the hot, dry centuries to come.

What happened to the Anasazi? The mummies help us discover how these people developed into a great civilization. But the mummies don't tell us why the

Anasazi left. Are there other clues preserved from the distant past that might help to solve this mystery?

In Chaco Canyon scientists have been able to study twenty-two pack-rat nests covering a period of 10,000 years. Pack rats lived in the caves before the Anasazi came and stayed after they left. Pack rats like to collect things, and they don't travel far. Everything they drag back to their nest comes from nearby. So anything found in a pack-rat nest, or pack-rat midden, as the scientists call it, comes from the same area as the Anasazi.

Over the centuries, generations of pack rats gathered feathers, cacti, sagebrush, juniper and pinecones, squash, twigs, insects, anything and everything that grew around the Anasazi. Then they hauled their "treasures" into the dry caves. As they deposited urine around the

Pack rats gathering cacti for their nest.

nest, the dry air of the caves turned the nest area into a clump that hardened like amber. The scientists called this amber rat and took it back to the lab to soak, pull apart, and study.

In the pack-rat middens from Chaco Canyon, the scientists discovered something very interesting. A thousand years ago there were juniper and piñon pines in the area. But over the next 200 years, during the peak of Anasazi activity, these two trees disappeared from the pack-rat record. The Anasazi needed trees for fuel and as a building material. As the canyon became treeless, the plants and animals that depended on them could no

A few items found in a pack-rat midden:

*Sap beetle about
3,000 years old.*

*Juniper twig about
9,500 years old.*

*Acacia thorns about
8,000 years old.*

*Saguaro seeds about
8,000 years old.*

longer survive. The valuable farmland would wash away. In a desert, every plant, animal, and drop of water is critical. Did the Anasazi become successful at the expense of their environment? They deserted their great cities after the trees disappeared.

The closest piñon pine today is a mile from Chaco Canyon, much too far for the pack rats to find. The junipers have not recovered in the area either. The loss seems to be permanent after the heavy use by the thriving Anasazi population.

Every situation where mummies can be found is always interesting and full of unusual clues about the past. But not everyone knows this. Mummies have been ground up, burned, robbed, and even forgotten. It has been very hard for mummies to get the respect they deserve.

MUMMIES
MISMANAGED

MILLIONS OF MUMMIES around the world would be shocked if they could see what has happened to their carefully preserved remains. When Mark Twain traveled to Egypt in 1904, he recorded that people no longer valued mummies and were using them to fuel the trains. "Pass out a king," yelled the engineer when he needed more steam. Since the mummified kings were covered with resin, they probably burned better than the common people. Thousands of other mummies were destroyed by grave robbers or flooded when the Aswan Dam was built along the Nile River.

Many other Egyptian mummies and almost all of those from the Canary Islands were apparently ground into "mummy powder" and sold as a medicine. Doctors

According to the writer Mark Twain, Egyptian mummies were used as fuel for trains.

prescribed the powder to Europeans in the Middle Ages for coughs, ulcers, headaches, bruises, and just about everything else. King Francis I of France never traveled without his pouch of ground-up mummy, just in case. By the 1500s, though, the supply of mummies was getting critically low. Clever merchants began to make fake mummies from slaves and others who had recently died, some from terrible diseases. When this new trade was discovered, laws were passed and doctors stopped prescribing mummy powder.

In Maine and Canada in the 1800s the linen wrappings around Egyptian mummies were made into paper. Because of all the resin, the sheets came out brown and were used to wrap up food in the markets. This practice

was stopped after an outbreak of cholera that people suspected came from the paper plant in Maine.

Mummies were also made into a brown pigment called *caput mortuum,* which is Latin for "dead head." It was a dark brown color used by artists to paint shadows. A version of *caput mortuum* is still available today, but it is made from entirely different ingredients.

In the early 1800s the British built mills just for grinding mummies into fertilizer for their cattle industry. Three hundred thousand Egyptian cat mummies were among those shipped for this purpose.

In 1875 a mummy of a child was discovered lying on a ledge in a Kentucky cave. The child was found with a bowl, pipe, moccasins, and arrow points. She was called "Little Alice" and spent years on exhibit in commercial caves and museums as a way to attract tourists coming

west on the trains. Finally in 1958 she

During the Middle Ages, mummies were ground into powder, which was thought to have healing powers.

was brought to the University of Kentucky for study and protection. There the child was found to be a nine- or ten-year-old boy who had died from internal injuries almost 2,000 years ago.

Little Alice, who had also been known as the Mammoth Cave Mummy and sometimes confused with another cave mummy called Little Fawn, was finally renamed Little Al. But this is not the only case of a mummy with a mistaken identity. Another mystery involves one that traveled back and forth across the country for sixty-six years and almost ended up on TV before he was finally identified and allowed to rest.

"Little Al" died almost 2,000 years ago.

THE OUTLAW WHO
WOULDN'T GIVE UP

LAUGH IN THE DARK FUN HOUSE, 1976. A television crew is filming an episode for the *Six Million Dollar Man* inside a fun house in Long Beach, California. When they set up the cameras in a dark corner, the director doesn't like the looks of the dummy dangling from the ceiling. It is sprayed with glow-in-the-dark paint and doesn't fit the scene.

A technician reaches up to remove the dummy. Plunk! The arm falls off. Everyone is shocked to see that this arm has a real bone. The dummy is a mummy, and no one knows who it is or how it got there. They call a medical examiner, and another mummy mystery begins.

As usual the mummy has clues. A look at the bones and tissues reveals a man about thirty years old with unhealthy lungs, probably from pneumonia. But he died from a gunshot wound in his chest. A copper bullet jacket still in the body turns out to be .32 caliber made between the 1830s and World War I.

Those are interesting clues but only the beginning. The examiner looks into the mummy's mouth. Inside is a 1924 penny and a ticket stub from "Louis Sonney's Museum of Crime, So. Main St., L.A." A check of driver's license records turns up Dan Sonney, who says that his father bought the mummy (they thought it was a dummy too) in the 1920s from an unknown source. Louis had a traveling road show called "The March of Crime" and charged people twenty-five cents to see the "outlaw who would never be captured live." When Louis died in 1949, the road show was put into storage until 1971. Then these items were bought by Spoony Singh, owner of the Hollywood Wax Museum.

Spoony thought the mummy was made from papier-mâché and sent it off to Mount Rushmore to be part of a haunted house. It was returned as "not being lifelike enough." Eventually the body lost its identity and ended up dangling at the fun house in front of the TV crew.

It takes only a few days to get this much information,

but questions still remain. Who was this man? The police want to identify the body. They keep looking and find an old partner of Louis Sonney's who remembers buying the mummy from a retired coroner in Tulsa, Oklahoma. The partner thinks the mummy had been a robber.

Then people in Oklahoma get involved in this mummy mystery. The history buffs search through

Elmer McCurdy, alias Frank Curtis, alias Frank Davidson, killed near Pawhuska, Okla, Oct. 7, 1911

The outlaw Elmer McCurdy, as discovered (top) and dressed to be buried (bottom). Western History Collections, University of Oklahoma Library.

libraries and state records and come up with a prime suspect: Elmer McCurdy, alias Elmer McCuardy, Elmer McAudry, Frank Curtis, and Frank Davidson. Profession? Outlaw. They find one final clue that only a mummy could solve. Elmer had a scar two inches long on the back of his right wrist.

Elmer's age and height match up with the mummy. And then, even though his skin is now hard and cracked, the two-inch scar can still be seen on the wrist just as described in the prison records.

Now that Elmer McCurdy is identified, the police manage to gather some details about how he died. As the story goes, he joined a gang that robbed a train in Kansas. The gang hoped to get several thousand dollars being sent as a payment to Indian tribes, but they picked the wrong train. Instead they got forty-six dollars and some whiskey. Elmer drank some of the whiskey and slept in a hayloft until the posse found him early the next morning. There was a gun battle, and three times Elmer was asked to give up. He refused every time and was eventually killed on October 7, 1911. Since no one claimed the body, the coroner preserved him in arsenic and for a nickel allowed the curious to take a peek at

Elmer, who became known as the "Bandit Who Wouldn't Give Up." After five years carnival owners posing as "relatives" claimed him and got him started in sideshows and circuses. Eventually he became an attraction without a name.

After he was identified in 1977, Elmer was given a eulogy on television and flown back to Oklahoma on a jet never seen in his lifetime. He is buried there under two cubic yards of concrete just in case anyone might think about digging him up and looking at him one more time.

When one considers all the damaged and destroyed mummies around the world, it is hard to imagine that there could be new mummy mysteries in the future. But preserved bodies are very enduring, and there are still some left to be found and others stored in safe conditions. With new technology to look for antibodies, DNA, and evidence of disease, mummies can give us more information than ever about the past.

MUMMIES
OF THE FUTURE

FORTUNATELY FOR FUTURE MUMMIES, we no longer use them for medicine, fertilizer, paint, or paper. Instead scientists are trying to gather new information from them without doing any harm.

Mummies today can be examined with X rays and CT scans and never be unwrapped or touched. The U.S. Navy provided an X ray big enough to examine boats so an Egyptian bull mummy could be studied. This mummy turned out to be a fake stuffed with rags, sticks, and bones from 200 B.C. But most mummies are full of valuable details, especially now that we can look closely at cells and DNA, a genetic code that is found in all living cells. Using powerful microscopes and new machinery, scientists can magnify and study cells of mummies.

From this, they can discover important information about the way ancient people lived.

Right now, scientists are trying to learn more about the devastating "Spanish flu" of 1918 that killed more than 20 million people around the world. Seven miners who died of the flu are helping them with this study.

We can now tell what's inside this mummy with X rays. It's an Egyptian hawk. The Field Museum, Chicago, neg. nos. 74996-A, 74996-B.

They were buried on a frozen Arctic island and preserved as mummies. So far studies have shown that the virus came into humans from pigs. Any new knowledge about this virus will help scientists design a better vaccine for this flu in case it ever comes back. Whenever we find a mummy with any health problems, research can help us unravel the mysteries of our modern health problems.

Because mummies are so important, scientists are looking for the best ways to preserve them. In 1900, when a mammoth mummy was reported in Siberia, it took a team of scientists three months to cross the tundra. They studied it when they arrived, but it was far too heavy for them to remove. It took ten men to haul out a piece of the hide. They fed the 26,000-year-old meat to their dogs. It was the best they could do, but today with helicopters and refrigerated vehicles, we can do better.

An unusual idea for protecting mummies comes from crispy potato chips. Potato chips are sealed into bags where the oxygen has been removed and replaced with nitrogen. This nitrogen bath keeps the chips fresh, crisp, and free of decay. In 1994 eleven Egyptian mummies were moved to cases filled with nitrogen to keep fungus and bacteria from damaging the bodies.

Many mysteries still remain that could be solved only by the future discovery of a new mummy. Consider the mammoth. This large creature used to live in Asia, Europe, and North America many thousands of years ago. Now it is extinct, and today we still do not understand fully what happened to these animals.

A few mummified mammoths have been found with food in their stomachs. It seems starvation was not the problem. Most mammoths have not been found with spear points in their bodies or other evidence of slaughter. Therefore it seems unlikely that they were overhunted.

The woolly mammoth first appeared in India about 3 million years ago and died out about 10,000 years ago.

Did a climate change make life impossible for the mammoth? Perhaps it was a disease or an infection that destroyed them. So far we just haven't found the right mummy to give us the answer. But someday we might.

Or maybe someone will find a mummy of the great auk. This seabird lived in cold northern seas and used its wings like flippers to dive after fish. Eventually the auk lost the ability to fly because it didn't need to fly in order to survive.

With its great success on the water, a problem showed up for this bird only in the spring, when it was time to nest. Most seabirds fly up to high cliffs, where they are protected. But the flightless great auk had to pull itself out of the sea like a walrus and lay its egg near the edge of the water. This method worked fine until the bird was discovered by hungry sailors out exploring the world. The bird was just about the size of a nice fat goose and easy for them to catch for dinner. The large eggs also became part of the menu. It didn't take long for the great auk to disappear.

The last two birds may have been killed in 1844 on an island near Iceland, and all that remains are a few stuffed specimens. There is so much that we do not know about this bird. For instance, how soon could the chicks swim? Did the young have white splotches on their faces like the adults? Did they have any special ways to survive the cold winter? Someday a great auk mummy may show up with skin and soft tissues to reveal information otherwise lost forever.

The frozen Arctic may be hiding other secrets. The folk song "Lord Franklin" gives us a clue about one of them:

> *In Baffin's Bay where the Whale-fish blow,*
> *The fate of Franklin no man may know.*
> *The fate of Franklin no tongue can tell,*
> *Lord Franklin along with his sailors do dwell.*

Sir John Franklin has never been found. His last resting place is still a mystery and may hold new clues about the Franklin Expedition. His ships haven't been found either. The Canadian armed forces conducted the latest search in 1967. Fifty-one men used aerial photography and formed a diving team with an underwater sled to see what they could discover. They didn't find much, but there are still a few clues in Inuit folklore that might lead a future expedition in new directions.

Another mummy that might make an appearance is

Cleopatra, who died in 30 B.C. She was the last queen of Egypt before the Romans took control. Since all Egyptian rulers were mummified, she and the Roman emperor Mark Anthony were probably mummified too. If so, they have never been found.

Today people are still interested in making mummies. In California scientists are using a new method to preserve bodies donated for research. After the bodies are dried out, the scientists inject and coat them with a plastic called silicone. These plastic mummies have no odor, last a long time, and can be reused. Because of this silicone protection, fewer cadavers are now required for scientific research. For people who prefer traditional methods, there is also a program in Florida that mummifies bodies using the best Egyptian techniques.

Since the 1960s there are three places in the United States where bodies, or just the heads, can be frozen for the future. A few hundred people have signed up. When they die, their bodies are quickly cooled and the blood replaced with a liquid that acts like antifreeze. They are slipped into a protective "mummy" sleeping bag and then stored with other bodies in a capsule at minus 310 degrees Fahrenheit (minus 190 degrees Celsius). Liquid nitrogen is continuously pumped through the capsule to keep them very cold. At some point the people who have signed up for *cryonic sleep* are hoping to be revived and then cured of whatever killed them. Right now this is not possible. These people are counting on the development of *nano robots,* tiny tools the size of cells that might be able to repair cell destruction that occurs during freezing. A tiny motor now exists with teeth the size of red blood cells. Scientists are looking for something even smaller that could be injected into the bloodstream to destroy viruses or clean out deposits of cholesterol and fat that can block arteries.

We have learned from John Torrington, the frozen mummy so well preserved from the Franklin Expedition, that much damage occurred to his body as he froze. Sharp ice crystals cut through the delicate membranes of his cells and turned them to mush. Because of the jagged edges of ice crystals, no large mammal has ever been frozen and then successfully revived by humans.

But survival after freezing is not unknown in nature. Insect larvae in the Arctic have a natural antifreeze that allows them to freeze during the winter and then revive in the spring thaw. This is why there are so many mos-

A wood frog, through a natural process, can survive freezing. Scientists are hoping to mimic this process in humans.

quitoes in Alaska. The wood frog also has this ability. Sometimes it gets caught in a shallow pond that freezes up so quickly the frog becomes frozen stiff. Its heart stops and so does its breathing. But during this freeze, the frog's liver produces an enormous amount of glucose, a simple sugar, that acts like antifreeze in the blood. This natural antifreeze allows water to freeze and melt in the frog's body without damage. It has taken the wood frog a hundred million years to adapt this process.

There are also fish in Antarctica with natural antifreeze. It protects them down to 28 degrees Fahrenheit (minus 2 degrees Celsius), which happens to be the temperature of the water. Without this protection there would be no fish in Antarctica.

Tiny human parts like corneas and sperm can withstand freezing, but nothing larger than that. If hearts and livers could be frozen for longer periods, many more organs would be available for transplant. Right now kidneys can be cooled and kept for three days. A liver survives only thirty-six hours and a heart or lung only about six hours. By studying animals that can survive freezing and mummies that cannot, we may come up with new transplant procedures. We might even develop better ways to deal with long journeys into space.

If we are going to keep looking for mummies, we might wonder just how long they can last. Insects and frogs protected in amber for millions of years still have their soft muscles, organs, and cells, even their DNA, preserved. Plant material from the environment is often sealed with them. Right now the oldest known mummy is a weevil encased in amber for 135 million years. And the oldest record of a flightless bird in North America was recently found in New Jersey amber. It is 90 million years old.

With this amount of preservation it is almost certain that more mummies will be found. Working with mummies is like being a good detective. As long as we know how to read the clues and preserve the scene, we will someday solve more mummy mysteries.

THE FINAL
MUMMY MYSTERIES

1. Now you are the archaeologist. You are in a dry cave in the southwest United States. And you discover this mummy. What is it?

Clues: In the same area you have already found yucca sandals, turkey feathers, a fur blanket, corn, squash, and woven blankets.

Brenda Z. Guiberson, permission National Park Service, Chaco Culture NHP Museum Collection.

2. You are walking along a seashore and find a lump of a strange substance. You can scratch it, burn it, and even see through it. It is not a stone. What is it? When you look closely, you can see a mummified insect inside.

Clue: It came from a tree millions of years ago.

Neg. no. 5758(2), courtesy Department of Library Services, American Museum of Natural History.

3. You find this bracelet buried near an Anasazi cave. It is made from a beautiful shell. You're in the desert. How do you explain the presence of the shell?

Clues: Macaw feathers and copper bells are also in the cave.

National Park Service, Chaco Culture NHP Museum Collection.

4. Now you are in the Arctic. You have just found a frozen mummified body that looks like this man. Who is he?

Clues: He is wearing a British Royal Navy uniform from the 1840s and has a knife in his pocket with the initials J. F.

Tacoma Public Library.

5. You are still in the frozen Arctic. Now you find a mummified bird about the size of a goose. A large speckled egg is also preserved. You have never seen anything like these. What bird have you found? How can you take a look inside the egg without destroying it?

Clues: The bird has white splotches on its face and short stubby wings.

6. You are given an opportunity to examine this mummy. Insects have eaten through the skin on her back, and you can see the lungs. How did she become mummified? What disease did this person have?

Clues: There are lumps on the lung tissue. The mummy weighs only twenty pounds.

Brenda Z. Guiberson, permission Ye Olde Curiosity Shop, Seattle.

Answers to questions:
1. Rabbit. 2. Amber. 3. Someone traded for it. 4. John Franklin. 5. An extinct great auk. X-ray the egg. 6. She dried out naturally. The disease she had was tuberculosis.

BIBLIOGRAPHY

Aliki. *Mummies Made in Egypt.* New York: HarperCollins, 1979.

Ayer, Eleanor H. *The Anasazi.* New York: Walker, 1993.

Baldwin, Gordon C. *The Riddle of the Past: How Archaeology Detectives Solve Prehistoric Puzzles from the Past.* New York: Norton, 1965.

Beattie, Owen, and John Geiger. *Buried in Ice.* London: Hodder and Stoughton, 1992.

————. *Frozen in Time.* New York: Dutton, 1987.

Betancourt, Julio L., and Thomas R. Van Devender. "Holocene Vegetation in Chaco Canyon, New Mexico." *Science* 6 (November 1981): 656–658.

Betancourt, Julio L., Thomas R. Van Devender, and Paul S. Martin, eds. *Packrat Middens: The Last 40,000 Years of Biotic Change.* Tucson: University of Arizona Press, 1990.

Black, Lydia T. "Some Problems in Interpretation of Aleut Prehistory." *Arctic Anthropology* 20.1 (1983): 49–78.

Brody, J. J. *Anasazi.* New York: Rizzoli International, 1990.

Cockburn, Aidan, and Eve Cockburn, eds. *Mummies, Disease and Ancient Cultures.* New York: Cambridge University Press, 1980.

Deem, James M. *How to Make a Mummy Talk.* Boston: Houghton Mifflin, 1995.

Duke, William. "Biology on Ice." *Discover* (August 1994): 36–41.

El Mahdy, Christine. *Mummies, Myth and Magic.* London: Thames and Hudson, 1989.

George, Angelo I. *Mummies, Catacombs, and Mammoth Cave.* Louisville: George Publishing, 1994.

Getz, David. *Frozen Man.* New York: Holt, 1994.

Grant, David Noble, ed. *New Light on Chaco Canyon.* Santa Fe: School of American Research, 1984.

Guthrie, R. Dale. *Frozen Fauna of the Mammoth Steppe: The Story of Blue Babe.* Chicago: University of Chicago Press, 1990.

Hall, Charles F. *Narrative of the Second Arctic Expedition.* Washington, DC: GPO, 1879.

Harris, Nathaniel. *Mummies: A Very Peculiar History.* New York: Franklin Watts, 1995.

Joyce, Christopher, and Eric Stover. *Witnesses from the Grave: The Stories Bones Tell.* New York: Ballantine, 1991.

Judd, Neil M. "The Pueblo Bonito Expedition of the National Geographic Society." *National Geographic* (March 1922): 323–331.

Judd, Neil M. "Pueblo Bonito, the Ancient." *National Geographic* (July 1923): 98–108.

Kane, Elisha Kent, M.D. *Arctic Explorations: The Second Grinnell Expedition in Search of Sir John Franklin.* Philadelphia: Childs & Peterson, 1853.

Lauber, Patricia. *Tales Mummies Tell.* New York: Crowell, 1985.

Lister, Robert H., and Florence C. Lister. *Chaco Canyon: Archaeology and Archaeologists.* Albuquerque: University of New Mexico Press, 1981.

McCracken, Harold. *God's Frozen Children.* Garden City, NY: Doubleday, 1930.

McHargue, Georgess. *Mummies.* New York: J. B. Lippincott, 1972.

Mountfield, David. *History of Polar Exploration.* New York: Dial, 1974.

Pääbo, Svante. "Ancient DNA." *Scientific American* (November 1993): 86–92.

Papanek, John L., ed. *People of the Ice and Snow.* Alexandria, VA: Time-Life Books, 1994.

Putnam, James. *Mummy.* New York: Knopf, 1992.

Thomson, Peggy. *Auks, Rocks and the Odd Dinosaur: Inside Stories from the Smithsonian's Museum of Natural History.* New York: Crowell, 1985.

Toufexis, Anastasia. "The Mummy's Tale." *Time,* 28 March 1994, 53.

Ubelaker, Douglas, and Henry Scammell. *Bones: A Forensic Detective's Casebook.* New York: HarperCollins, 1992.

Watson, Don. "Ancient Cliff Dwellers of Mesa Verde." *National Geographic* (September 1948): 349–376.

Weyer, Edward Moffat, Jr. "An Aleutian Burial," in *Anthropological Papers.* New York: American Museum of Natural History, 1929.

Wilcox, Charlotte. *Mummies and Their Mysteries.* Minneapolis: Carolrhoda, 1993.

Woodman, David C. *Unraveling the Franklin Mystery: Inuit Testimony.* Montreal: McGill-Queen's University Press, 1991.

Wright, Karen. "Revelations of Rat Scat." *Discover* (September 1993): 64–71.

Zimmer, Carl. "Carriers of Extinction." *Discover* (July 1995): 28–30.

INDEX

(Page numbers in *italic* refer to illustrations.)